UNDERSTANDING
PRESIDENTIAL ELECTIONS

BY MATT BOWERS

AMICUS | AMICUS INK

Sequence is published by Amicus and Amicus Ink
P.O. Box 1329, Mankato, MN 56002
www.amicuspublishing.us

Library of Congress Cataloging-in-Publication Data
Names: Bowers, Matt, author.
Title: Understanding presidential elections / by Matt Bowers.
Description: Mankato, Minnesota : Amicus, [2020] | Series: Sequence American
  Government | Audience: Grades: K to Grade 3. | Includes webography. |
  Includes index.
Identifiers: LCCN 2018033779 (print) | LCCN 2018035064 (ebook) |
  ISBN 9781681517568 (pdf) | ISBN 9781681516745 (Library Binding) |
  ISBN 9781681524603 (Paperback)
Subjects: LCSH: Presidents--United States--Election--Study and teaching
  (Elementary).
Classification: LCC JK528 (ebook) | LCC JK528 .B69 2020 (print) | DDC
  324.60973--dc23
LC record available at https://lccn.loc.gov/2018033779

Editor: Alissa Thielges
Designer: Veronica Scott
Photo Researcher: Holly Young

Photo Credits: Shutterstock/Sandra Matic cover; Getty/Chip Somodevilla 5; Getty/Saul Loeb, AFP 6–7; AP/Jacquelyn Martin 9; AP/Alex Driehaus 10–11; iStock/adamkaz 13; Getty/John Sommers II 14–15; AP/Bill Clark, CQ Roll Call 17; Shutterstock/a katz 18; Newscom/Reuters, Carlos Barria 20–21; Alamy/Autumn Payne, Sacramento Bee, zumapress.com 22; AP/Chris Maddaloni, CQ Roll Call 24–25; 270towin.com 25; AP/Julie Jacobson 26; Alamy/nagelestock.com 29

Printed in the United States of America

HC 10 9 8 7 6 5 4 3 2 1
PB 10 9 8 7 6 5 4 3 2 1

The U.S. President

U.S. citizens have an awesome power. They have the right to vote! Every four years, they choose a president. It is an important decision. The president leads the executive branch of the U.S. government. This is a big role to fill. It includes commanding the military, vetoing bills, and choosing judges.

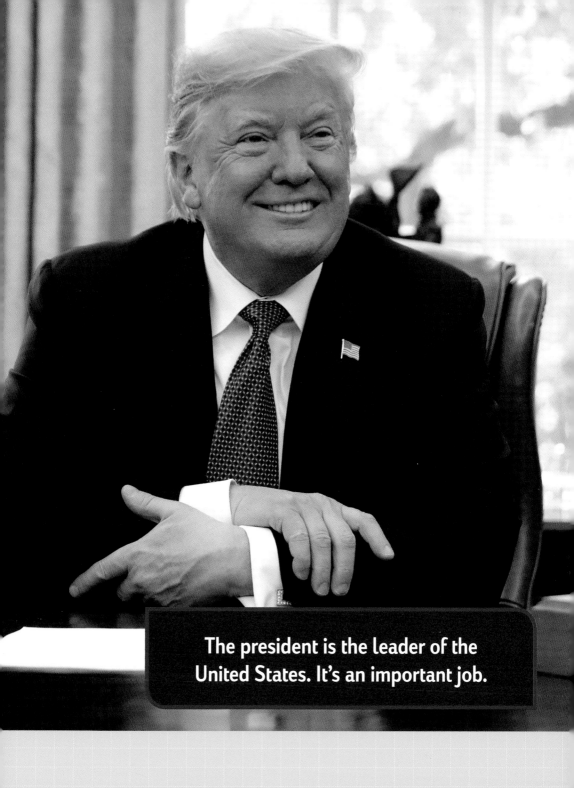

The president is the leader of the United States. It's an important job.

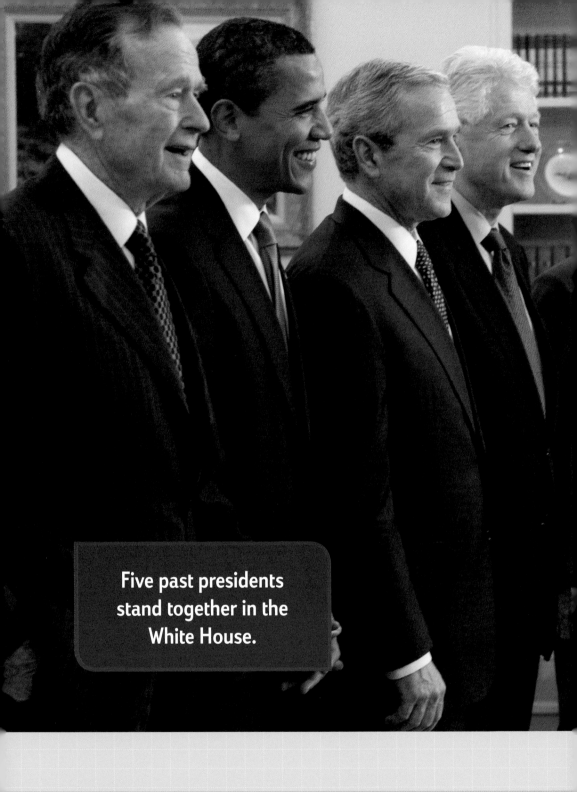

Five past presidents
stand together in the
White House.

LOADING...LOADING...LOADING...

Can anyone run for president?
No. There are three requirements.
First, a person must be born as
a citizen of the United States.
Second, they must be at least 35
years old. And last, they must have
lived in the United States for at
least 14 years.

So how are presidents elected?
Let's look at a typical election.

Choosing a Candidate

It all begins many months before Election Day. People start announcing their run for president. This can be a big event. The media is there. All their cameras flash. The **candidate** gives a speech. They say why they are running. They talk about what they will do if they are elected. Voters listen.

Candidates announce they are running for U.S. president.

MONTH 1

LOADING...LOADING...

Bernie Sanders announces his run for president in 2016.

Candidates announce they are running for U.S. president.

MONTH 1 ⟶

...ING...LOADING...

Candidates build their campaigns.

Next, the **campaigns** begin. There is so much to do! The candidates build their teams. Staff is hired. Offices are set up. The teams travel around the country. The candidates give speeches and meet voters. They talk about their plans. Voters ask them questions.

A campaign costs a lot. People give money to help their favorite candidate.

People go to rallies for their favorite candidates.

By fall, there are many candidates. Most are in a **political party**. In the United States, there are two main parties. One is the Democratic Party. The other is the Republican Party.

There are many other parties, too. They are called "third parties." Some candidates are independents. They do not belong to a party.

A candidate often shares the same ideas as their political party.

Candidates announce they are running for U.S. president.

Candidates campaign across the country, gaining support.

MONTH 1 ———————⟶ MONTH 8

. . . LOADING . . .

Candidates build their campaigns.

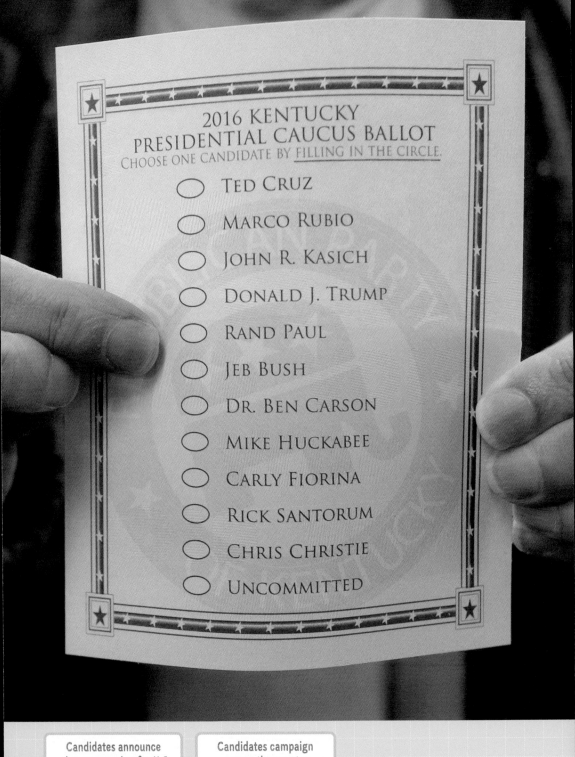

2016 KENTUCKY PRESIDENTIAL CAUCUS BALLOT
CHOOSE ONE CANDIDATE BY <u>FILLING IN THE CIRCLE.</u>

○ TED CRUZ

○ MARCO RUBIO

○ JOHN R. KASICH

○ DONALD J. TRUMP

○ RAND PAUL

○ JEB BUSH

○ DR. BEN CARSON

○ MIKE HUCKABEE

○ CARLY FIORINA

○ RICK SANTORUM

○ CHRIS CHRISTIE

○ UNCOMMITTED

Candidates announce they are running for U.S. president.

Candidates campaign across the country, gaining support.

MONTH 1 ⟶ MONTH 8   MONTH 11   ᴀᴅᴵɴɢ . . .

Candidates build their campaigns.

Candidates compete in primaries and caucuses.

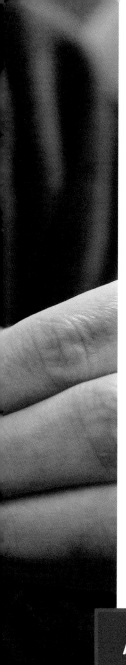

Each party chooses one candidate to support. This is not an easy process. A lot of states hold **primary elections**. This is an election that states hold for each party. Candidates compete for the most **delegates**. These are people who choose the party's candidate. Some states hold **caucuses**. In these meetings, party members choose the delegates.

A party can have more than 10 candidates. A caucus helps narrow the choices.

LOADING... LOADING... LOADING...

After the primaries, each party has a national convention. These are big meetings. Delegates select the party's candidate for president. A running mate is named, too. This is the vice presidential candidate. There are a lot of speeches. The crowd cheers. It is a big rally! At last, each party has one candidate for president. Now the **general election** season begins.

Candidates announce they are running for U.S. president.

Candidates campaign across the country, gaining support.

Parties hold national conventions and choose one candidate.

MONTH 1 ⟶ MONTH 8 MONTH 11 MONTH 17

Candidates build their campaigns.

Candidates compete in primaries and caucuses.

Donald Trump speaks at the Republican National Convention in 2016. He was the party's candidate.

LOADING...LOADING...LOADING...

Hillary Clinton gives a speech. She was the Democratic candidate in 2016.

Candidates announce they are running for U.S. president.	Candidates campaign across the country, gaining support.	Parties hold national conventions and choose one candidate.

MONTH 1 ⟶ MONTH 8 　　MONTH 11 　　MONTH 17 　　MONTH 18

Candidates build their campaigns.	Candidates compete in primaries and caucuses.	**Candidates compete for votes in the general election.**

Campaigning for Votes

The general election takes place in November. The candidates have a few months to campaign. They go all over the nation. It is a very busy time. The candidates share their ideas. They go to rallies. They talk to voters. There are lots of ads about them. The candidates try to gain people's votes.

People discuss the candidates. Some people have decided how they will vote. Others have not. They are called undecided voters.

During this time, the candidates take part in **debates**. Here the candidates take turns answering questions. They talk about their plans as president. They discuss problems in the nation and how they will fix them. Maybe one question is about schools. Another is on lowering taxes. These debates help voters decide how they will vote.

Candidates announce they are running for U.S. president.

Candidates campaign across the country, gaining support.

Parties hold national conventions and choose one candidate.

MONTH 1 — MONTH 8 MONTH 11 MONTH 17 MONTH 18

Candidates build their campaigns.

Candidates compete in primaries and caucuses.

Candidates compete for votes in the general election.

Donald Trump and Hillary Clinton shake hands before a 2016 debate.

Candidates participate in debates.

OADING...LOADING...

Voting time! This woman puts a sticker on to show that she has voted.

Candidates announce they are running for U.S. president.

Candidates campaign across the country, gaining support.

Parties hold national conventions and choose one candidate.

MONTH 1 ⟶ MONTH 8   MONTH 11   MONTH 17   MONTH 18

Candidates build their campaigns.

Candidates compete in primaries and caucuses.

Candidates compete for votes in the general election.

Time to Vote!

In November, it's finally Election Day! People vote for the next U.S. president. Across the nation, voters go to the **polls**. They vote for their favorite candidate. All voters are part of the **popular vote**. But the final vote for president is done by a group of electors from each state. This process is called the **electoral college**.

Candidates participate in debates.

MONTH 19   MONTH 21   NG . . . LOADING . . .

People cast their votes on Election Day in November.

States with more people have more electors. In most states, the candidate who wins the state's popular vote gets all the state's electoral votes. Electors vote in December. Electoral maps show the results. When a candidate wins, they get the electoral votes in that state. There are 538 votes in total. The candidate who gets 270 or more votes wins!

Candidates announce they are running for U.S. president.

Candidates campaign across the country, gaining support.

Parties hold national conventions and choose one candidate.

MONTH 1 ⟶ MONTH 8   MONTH 11   MONTH 17   MONTH 18

Candidates build their campaigns.

Candidates compete in primaries and caucuses.

Candidates compete for votes in the general election.

2016 Actual

State	Electoral Votes
MA	11
RI	4
CT	7
NJ	14
DE	3
MD	10
DC	3

270 TO WIN

An electoral map of 2016 shows which party won each state's votes. Red states voted Republican. Blue states voted Democratic.

Candidates participate in debates.

Electors from each state vote in December.

MONTH 19   MONTH 21   MONTH 22

LOADING...

People cast their votes on Election Day in November.

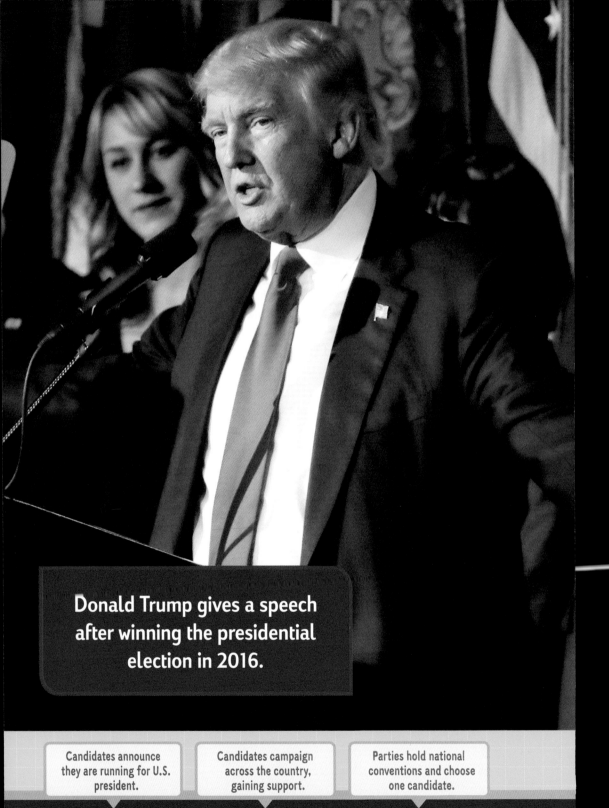

Donald Trump gives a speech after winning the presidential election in 2016.

| Candidates announce they are running for U.S. president. | Candidates campaign across the country, gaining support. | Parties hold national conventions and choose one candidate. |

MONTH 1 ⟶ MONTH 8   MONTH 11   MONTH 17   MONTH 18

| Candidates build their campaigns. | Candidates compete in primaries and caucuses. | Candidates compete for votes in the general election. |

The Nation's New President

After the votes are in, the winner is announced. Hooray! The nation has elected a new president! This person is called the **president-elect**. They prepare to take over the job in January. Until then, there is a lot to do. The president-elect works with a transition team to get ready.

Candidates participate in debates.

Electors from each state vote in December.

MONTH 19   MONTH 21   MONTH 22   MONTH 22   DING . . .

People cast their votes on Election Day in November.

The president-elect prepares to be president.

Inauguration Day is on January 20. This is when control transfers peacefully from the old president to the new president. At the Capitol, the new president takes an oath of office. This is a promise to protect the U.S. Constitution.

Presidents can serve up to two four-year terms. About halfway through the term, new candidates announce they are running for president. Then the process starts over again.

Candidates announce they are running for U.S. president.

Candidates campaign across the country, gaining support.

Parties hold national conventions and choose one candidate.

MONTH 1 ——————→ MONTH 8   MONTH 11   MONTH 17   MONTH 18

Candidates build their campaigns.

Candidates compete in primaries and caucuses.

Candidates compete for votes in the general election.

Fireworks go off over the U.S. Capitol building. There is a new president!

Candidates participate in debates.

Electors from each state vote in December.

Inauguration Day is held on January 20.

MONTH 19   MONTH 21   MONTH 22   MONTH 22   MONTH 23

People cast their votes on Election Day in November.

The president-elect prepares to be president.

29

Glossary

campaign The work candidates and their teams do to try to win an election.

candidate Someone who is trying to be elected.

caucus A meeting where members of a political party select delegates to attend a convention.

debate A public discussion between two or more people where candidates share ideas and plans and answer questions.

delegate A person who attends a political party's national convention and votes for the party's nominee for president.

electoral college A group of leaders from each state who officially elect the president and vice president.

general election An election where candidates for a political position, such as president, are voted on.

political party An organization of people with similar political ideas that works to win elections.

polls Places where people vote on Election Day.

popular vote The total number of votes cast by voters.

president-elect A new president who has won the general election but has not started serving yet.

primary election An election to choose the main candidate of each political party.

Read More

Klepeis, Alicia Z. *Understanding the Electoral College.* New York: Rosen Publishing, 2018.

Davis, Todd and Marc Frey. *The New Big Book of U.S. Presidents.* Philadelphia: Running Press Kids, 2017.

Gunderson, Jessica. *Understanding Your Role in Elections.* North Mankato, Minn.: Capstone, 2018.

Ford, Jeanne Marie. *How Elections Work.* North Mankato, Minn.: The Child's World, Inc., 2016.

Websites

Ben's Guide – The What and Who of Elections
https://bensguide.gpo.gov/what-and-who-of-elections-app

Library of Congress | Elections...the American Way
http://www.loc.gov/teachers/classroommaterials/ presentationsandactivities/presentations/elections/ election-process.html

Miller Center – U.S. Presidents
https://millercenter.org/president

Index

About the Author

Matt Bowers is a writer and illustrator who lives in Minnesota. When he's not writing or drawing, he enjoys skiing, sailing, and going on adventures with his family. He hopes readers will continue to learn about government and be leaders in their communities.